AF576603

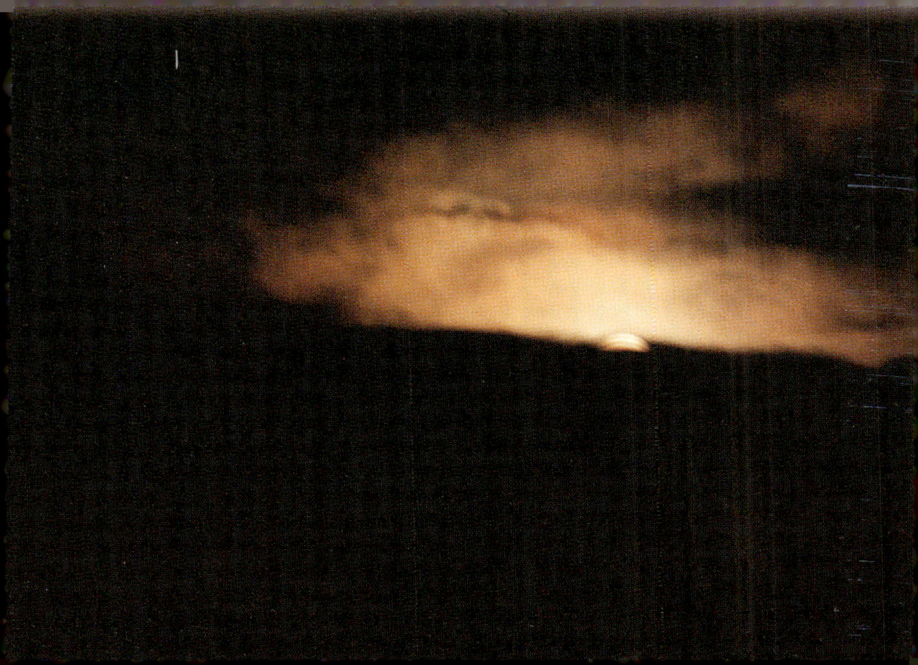

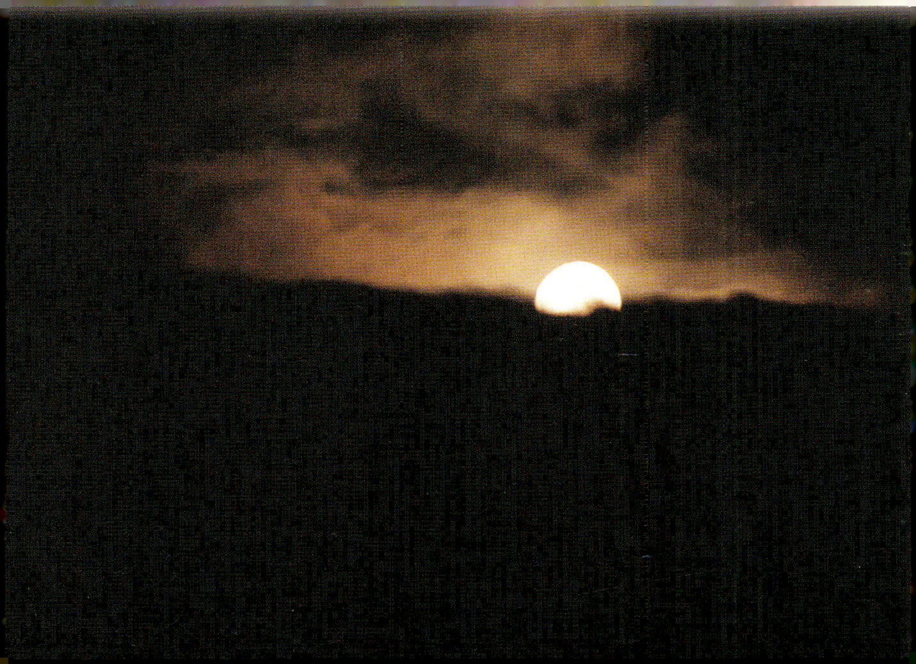

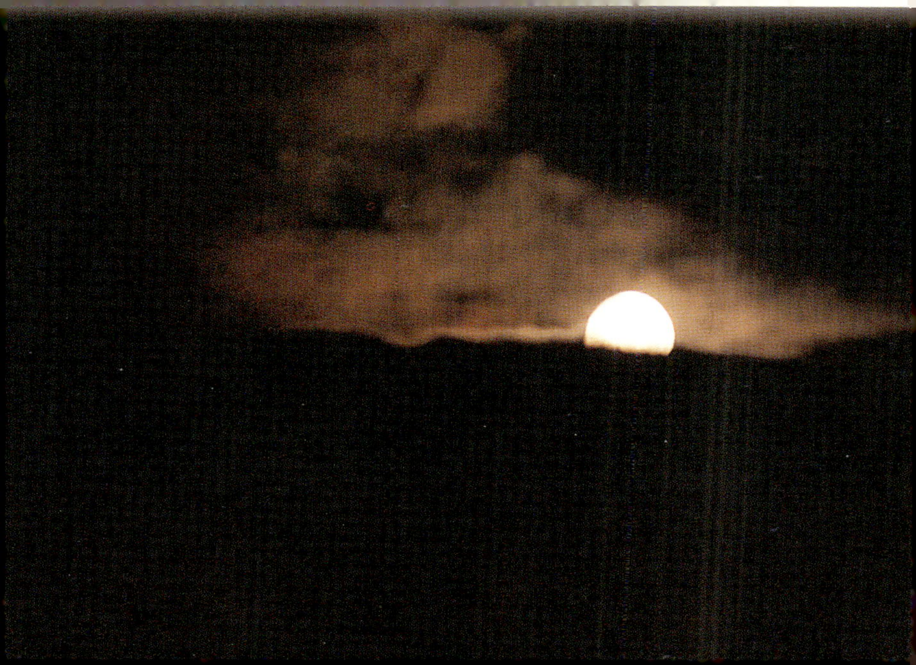

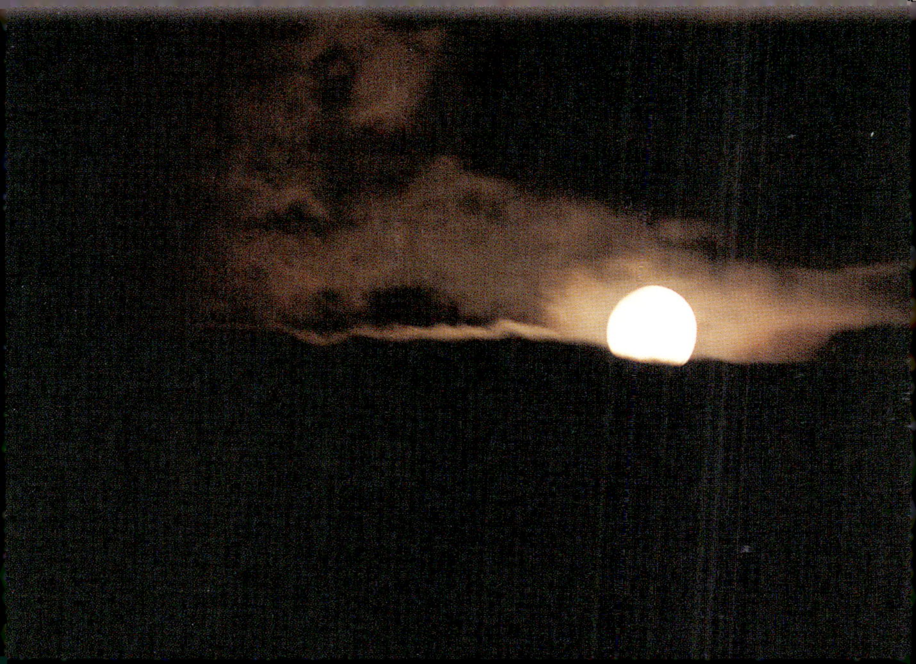

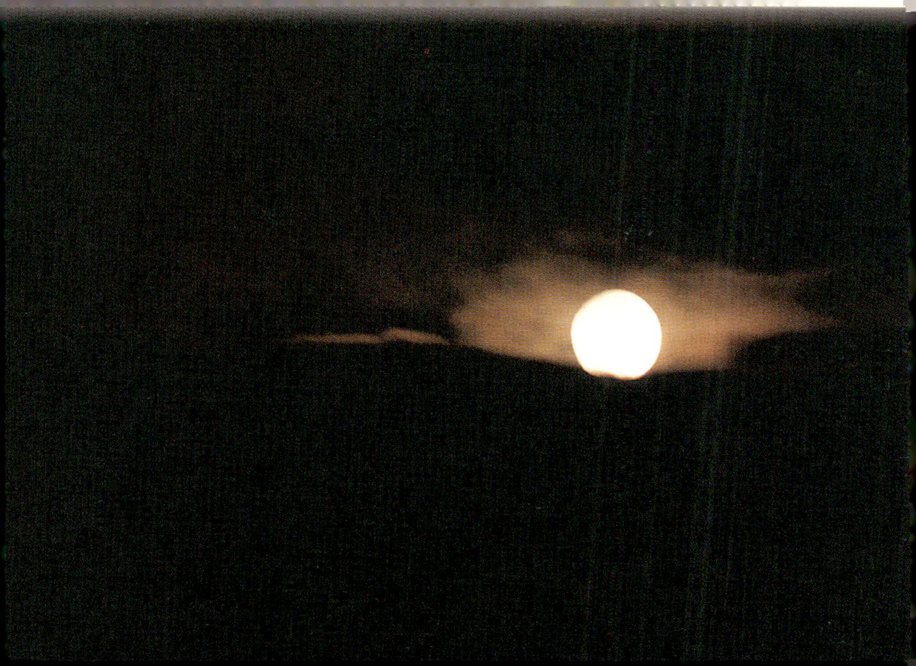

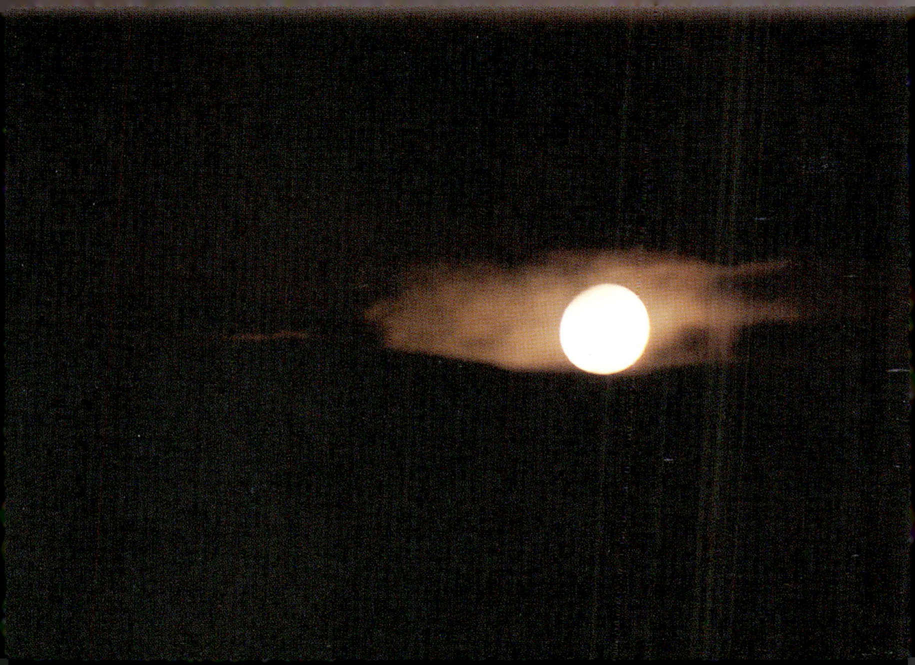

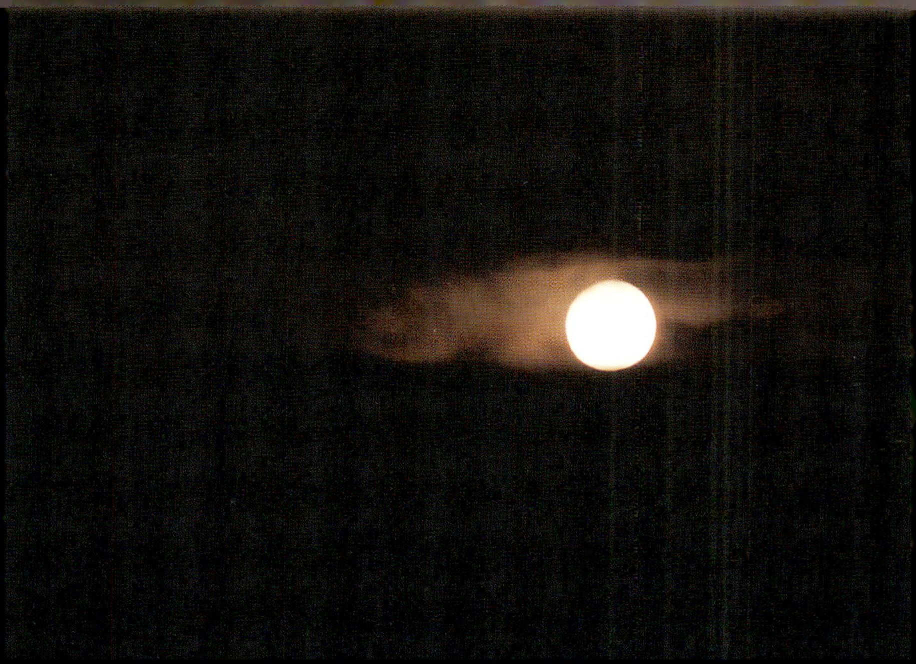

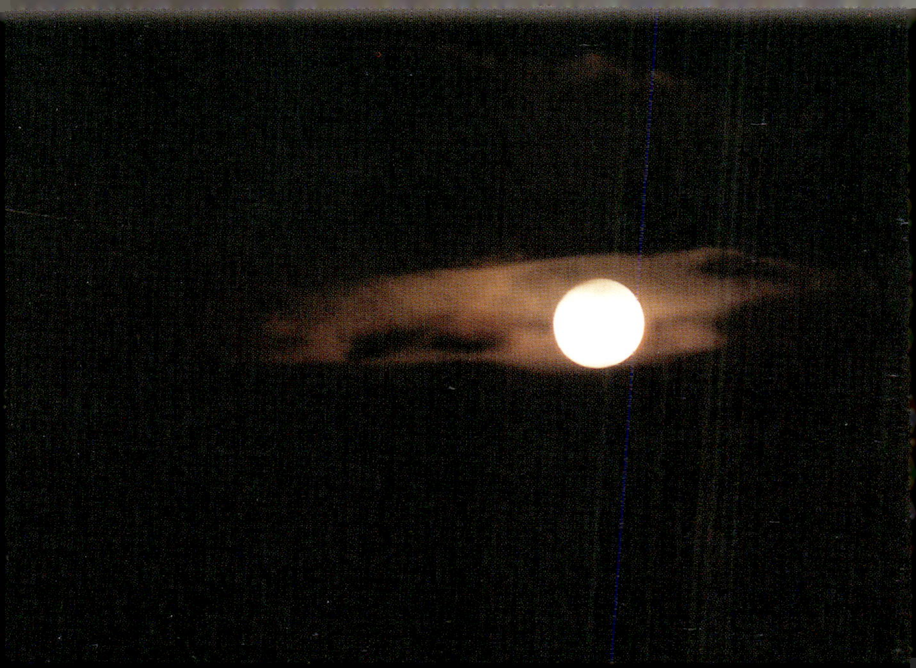

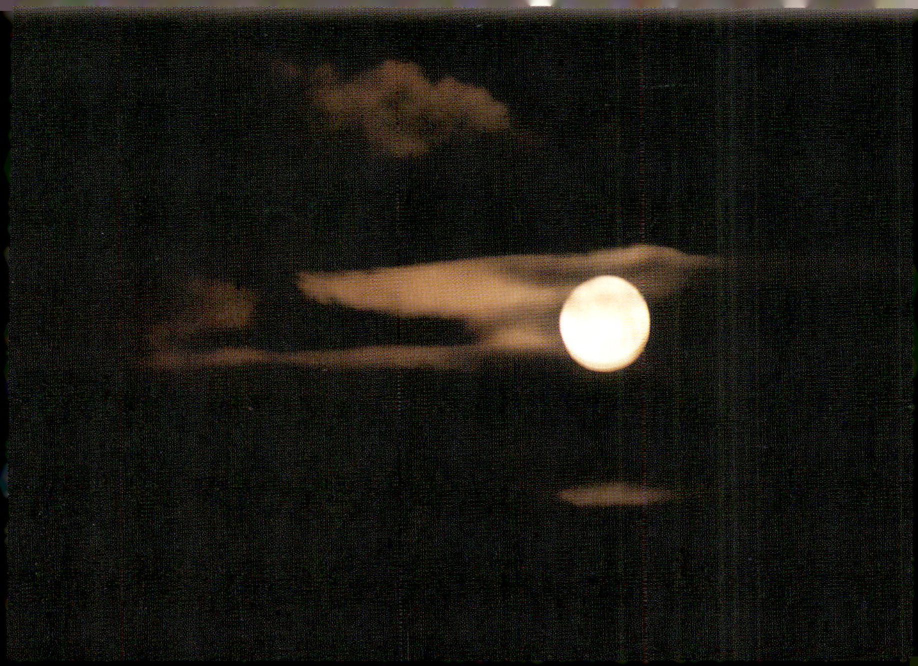

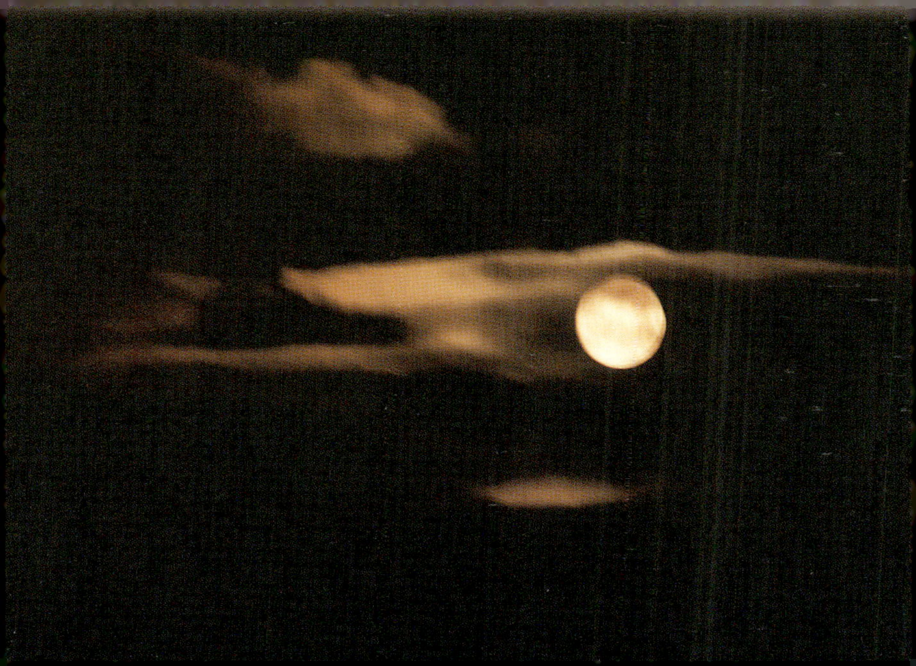

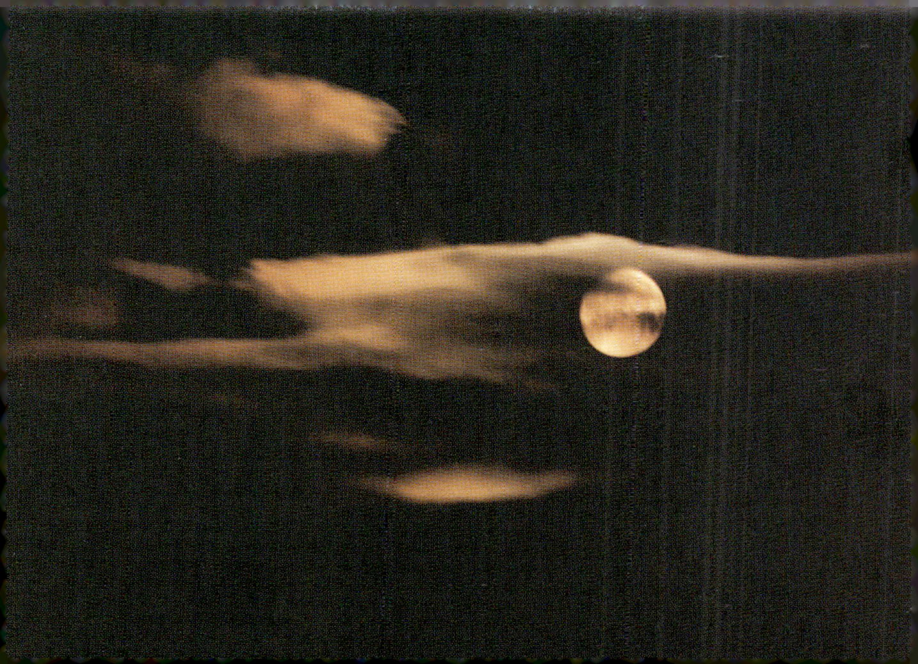

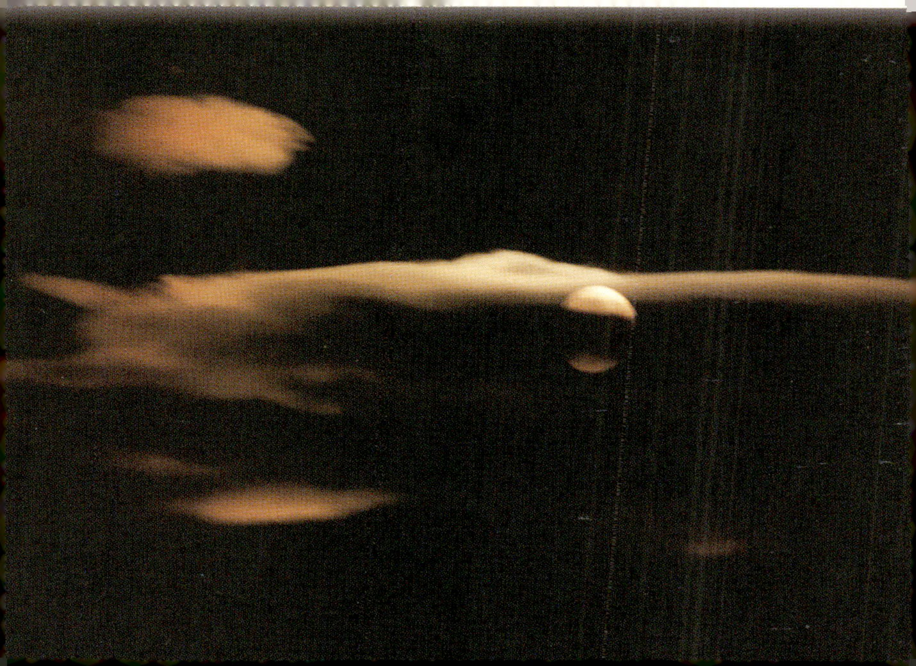

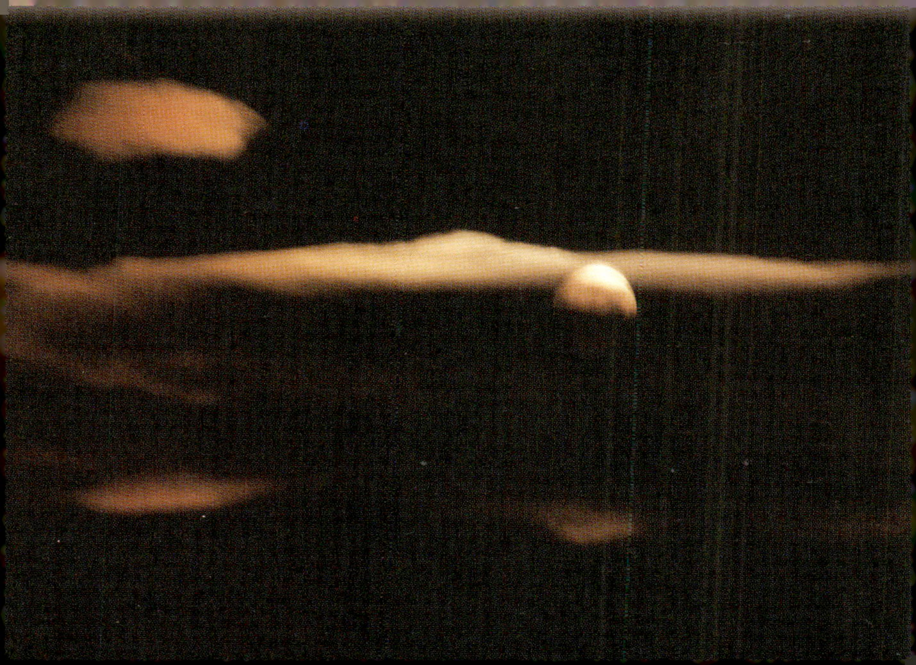

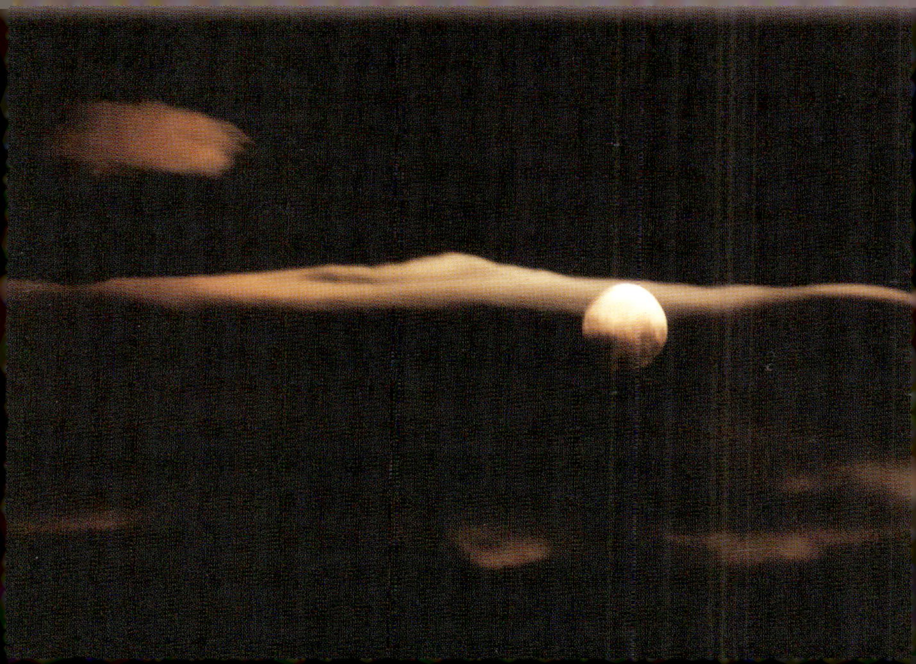

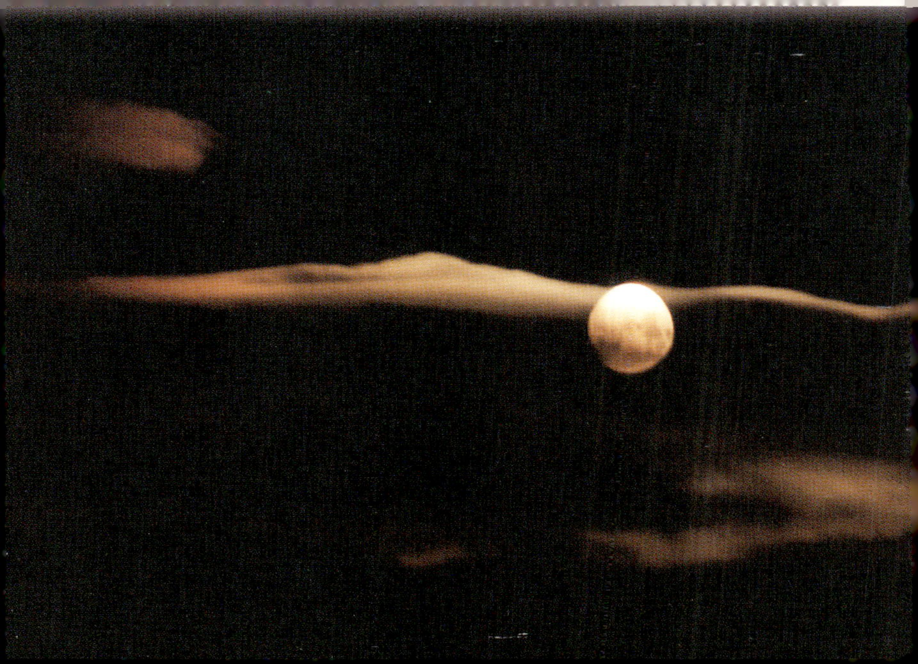

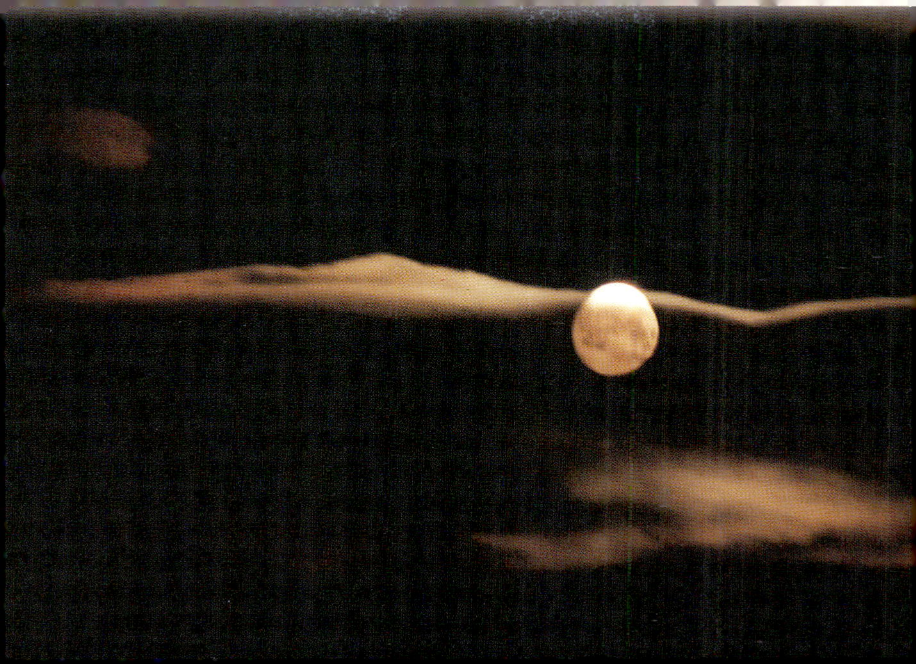

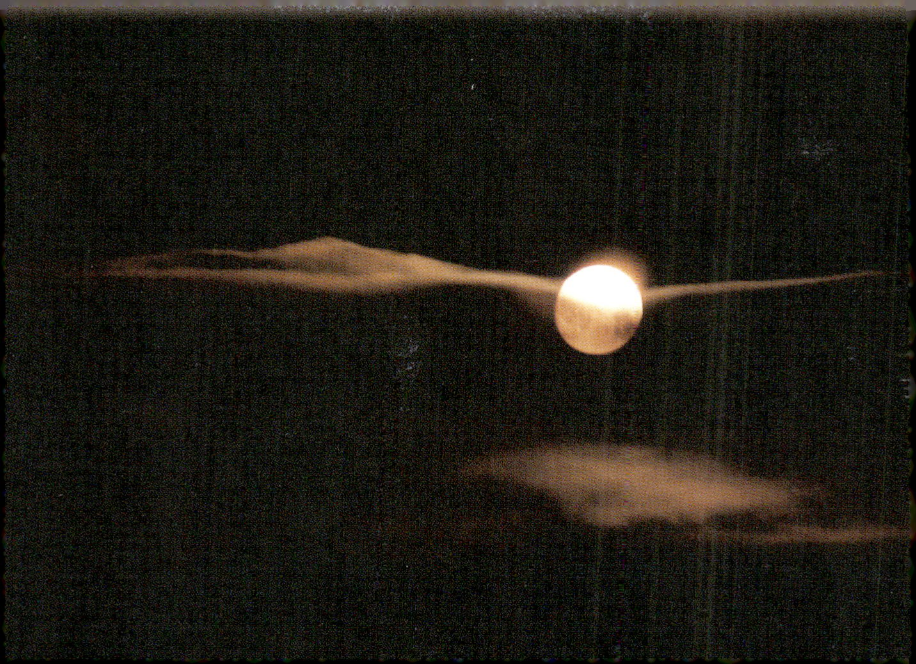

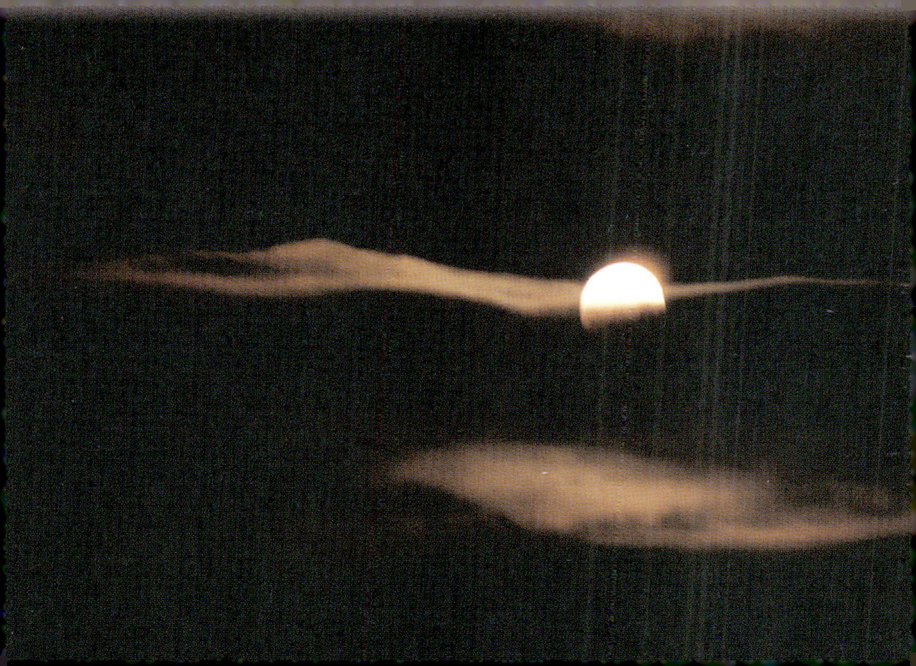

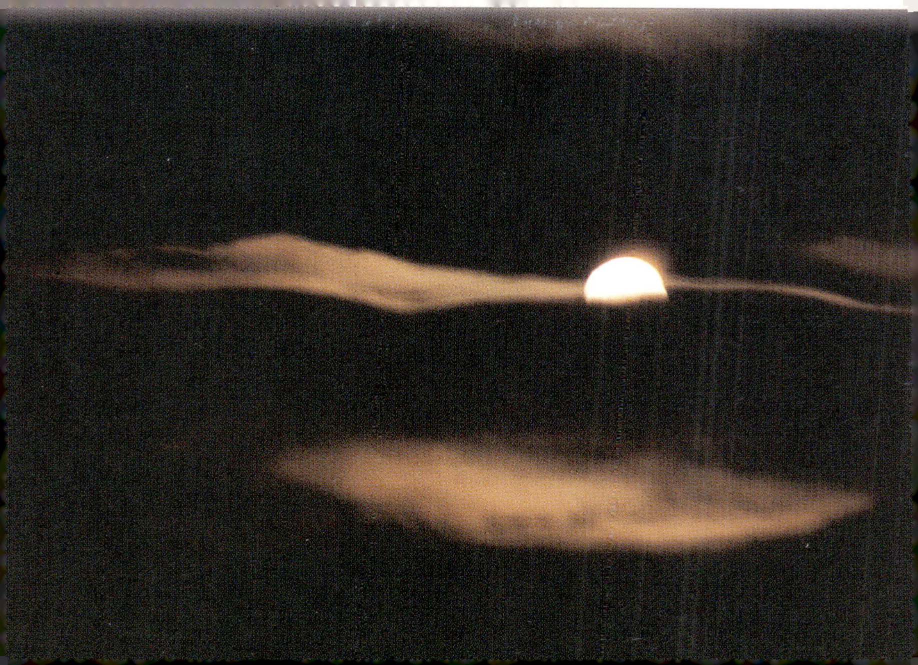

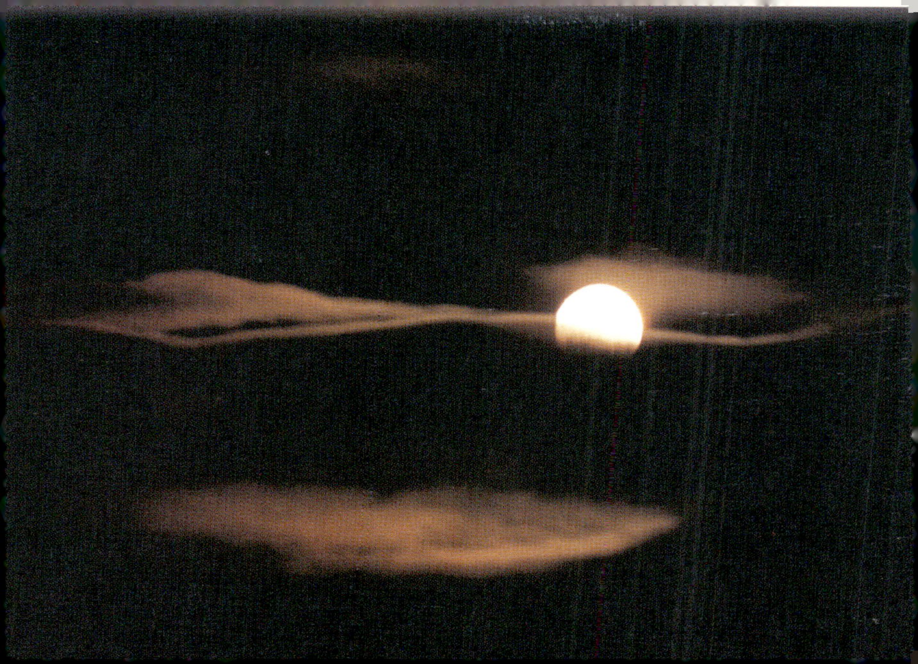

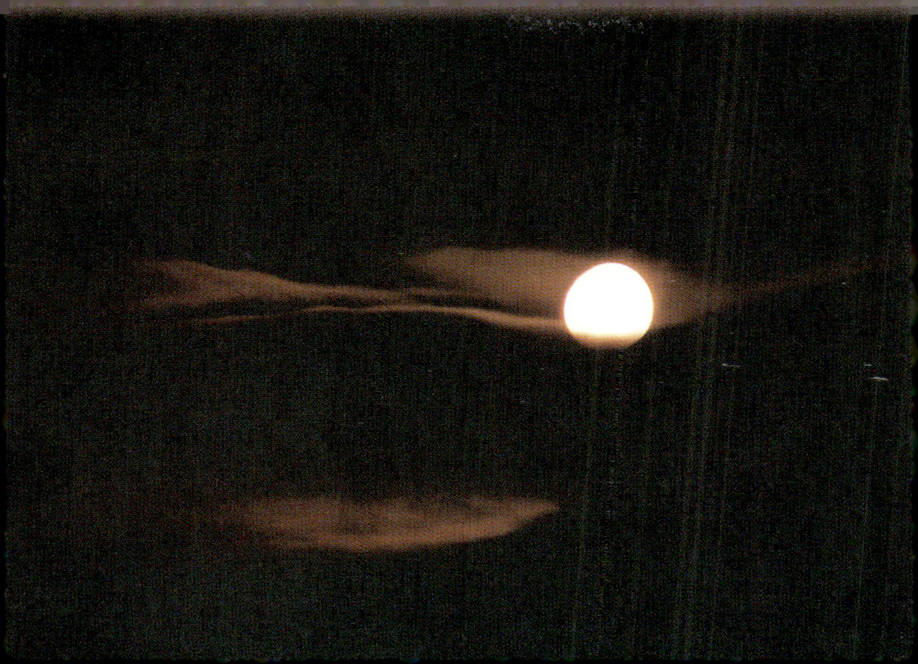

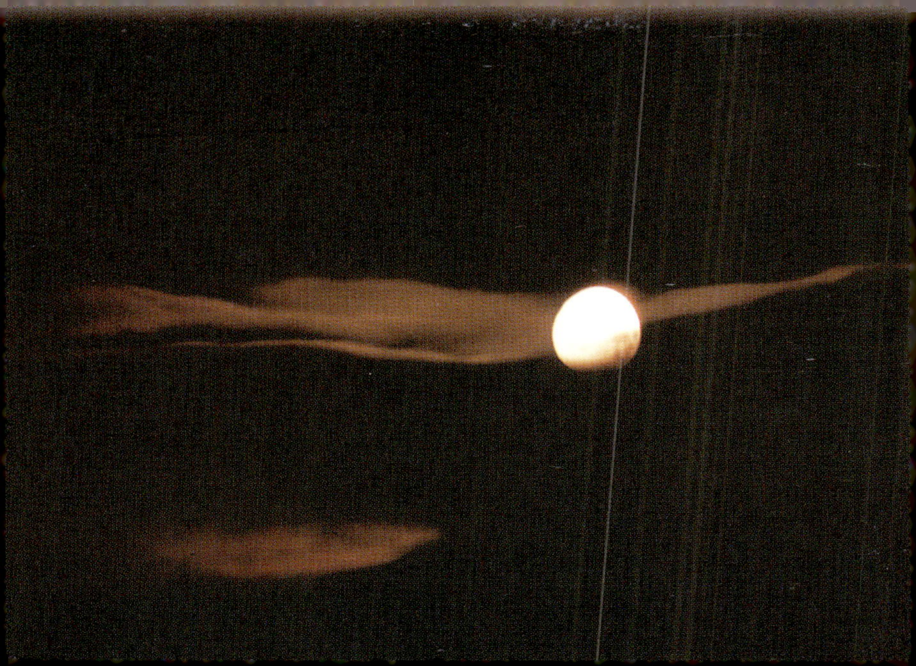

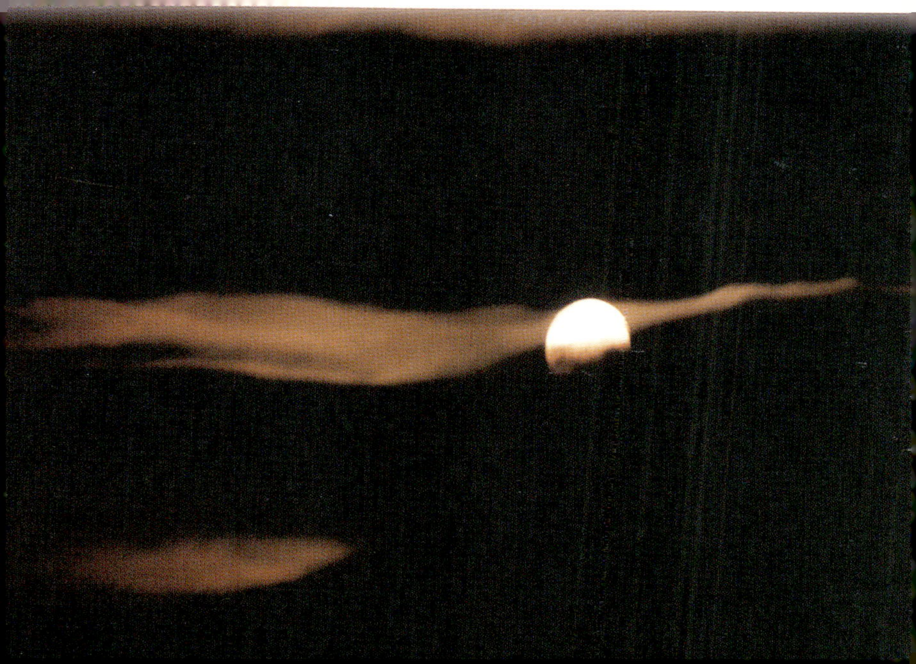

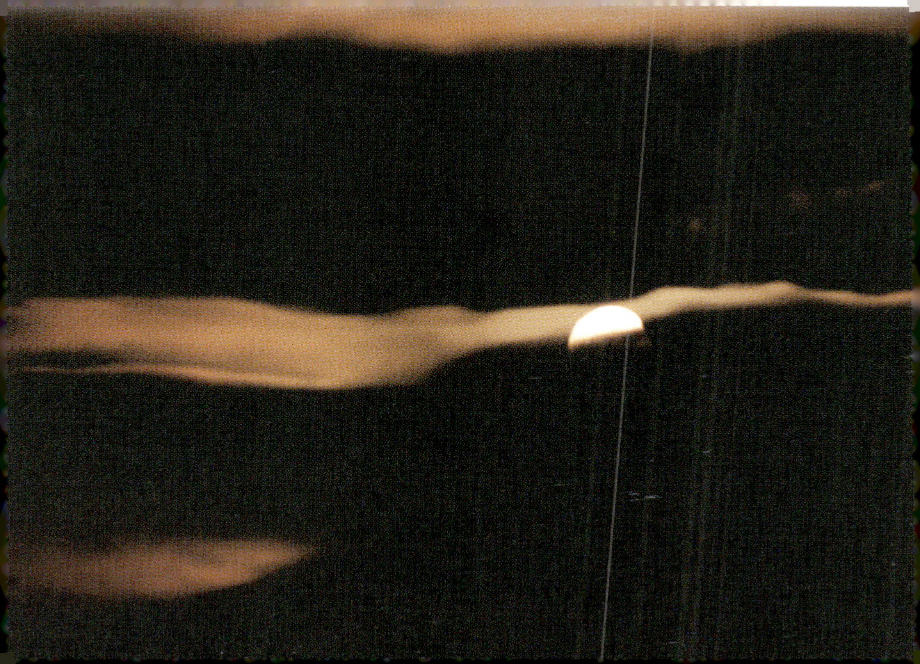

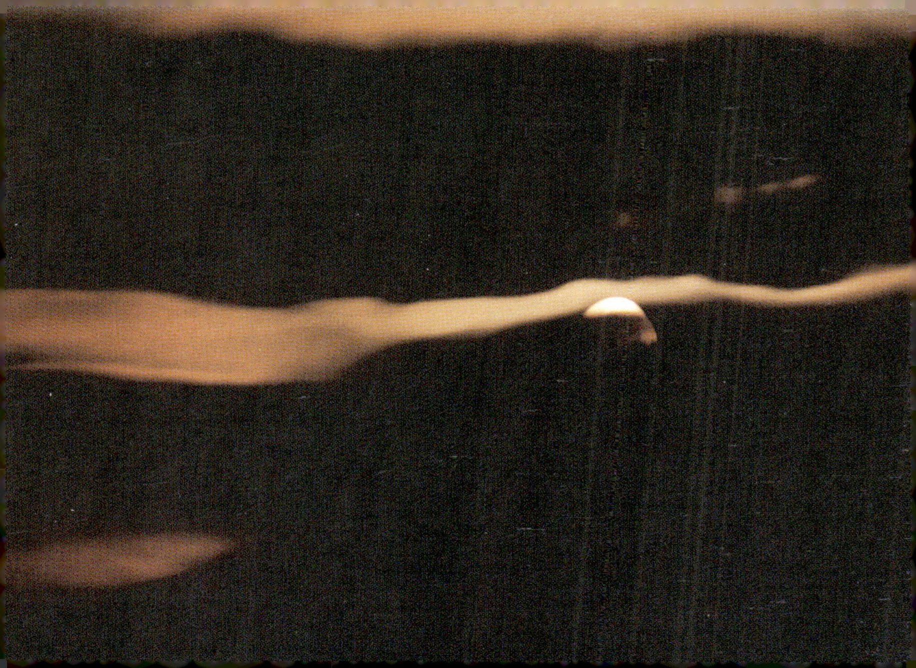

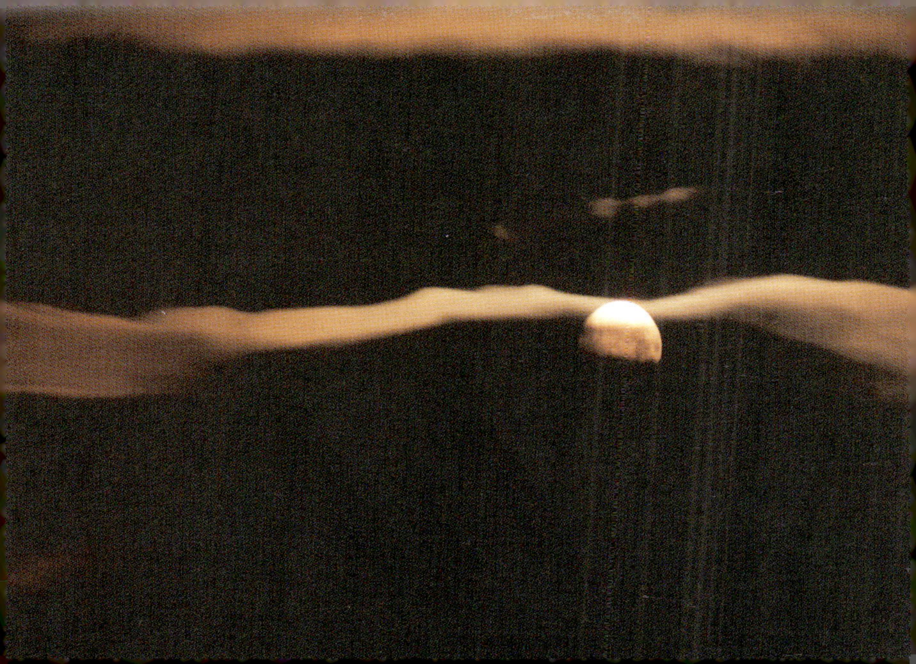

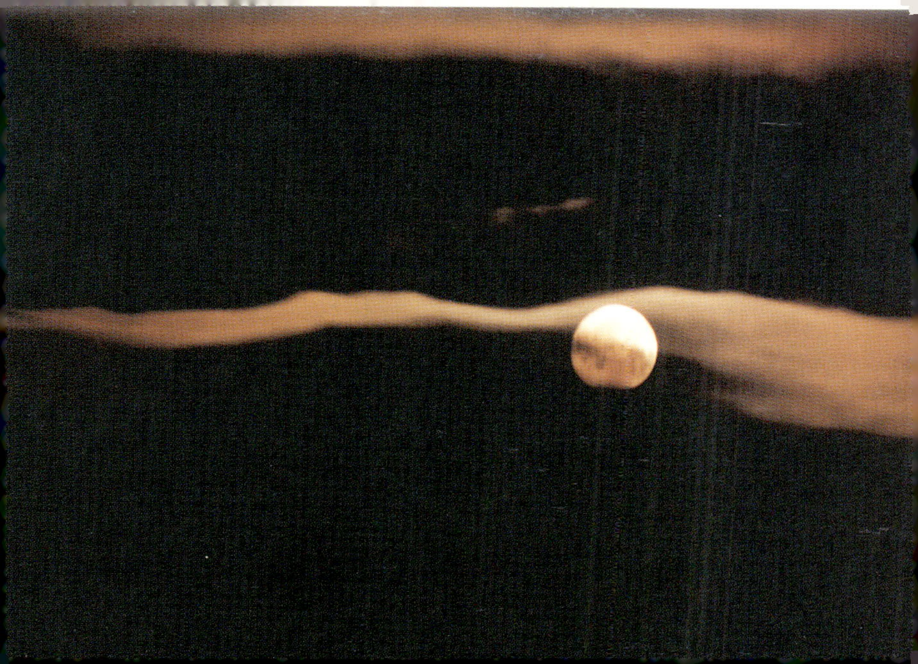

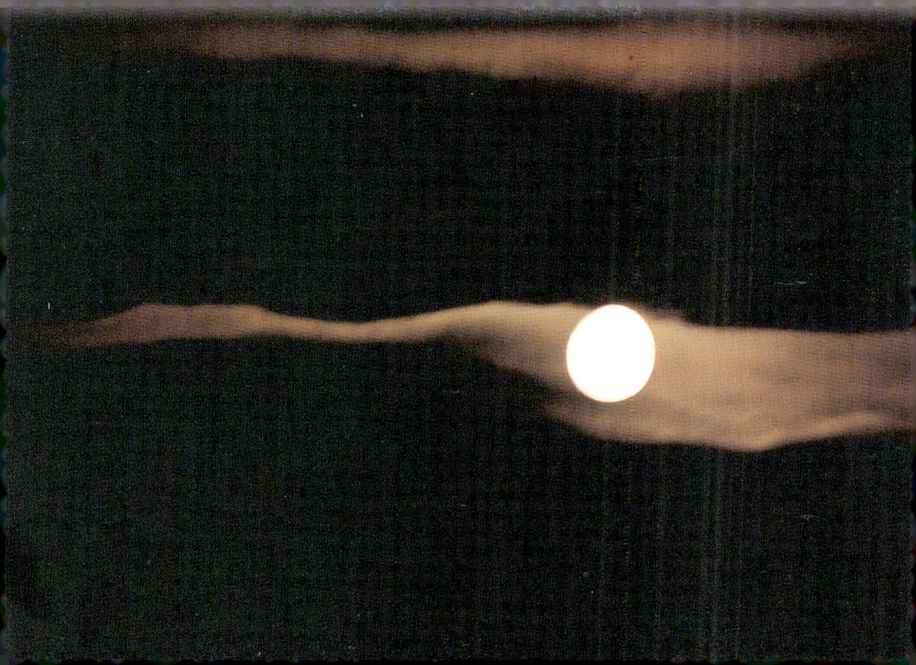

ASK YOUR LOCAL BOOK SELLER FOR THESE OTHER DONALD VERGER TITLES

• Best Friends • Demolition • Drawbridge •
• First Light • Rearview • Waves •

OR FOR A FULL CATALOG OF ANIMATED PUBLICATIONS, CONTACT

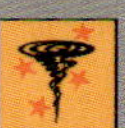

Designs for Discovery Press
(800) 566-6868

Photographs by Donald B. Verger
Westerly, Rhode Island
Cover Design by Toby S. Chaudhuri

First Edition, August, 1995
Printed in the USA

Library of Congress Cataloging-in-Publishing D
Verger, Donald B.
Moondance/Donald B. Verger
95-70054
ISBN 1-887-716-03-3

FOR MY SISTER LINDA, A TERRIFIC AND TALENTED HUMAN BEING